Starting Your Own
Import/Export Business

Guide to
Starting Your Own
Import/Export
Business

By
Karen Offitzer

A Citadel Press Book
Published by Carol Publishing Group

A Citadel Press Book
Published by Carol Publishing Group
Citadel Press is a registered trademark of Carol
Communications, Inc.

Editorial Offices: 600 Madison Avenue, New York, N.Y. 10022
Sales & Distribution Offices: 120 Enterprise Avenue, Secaucus,
N.J. 07094
In Canada: Canadian Manda Group, P.O. Box 920, Station U, Toronto,
Ontario M8Z 5P9

Queries regarding rights and permissions should be addressed
to Carol Publishing Group, 600 Madison Avenue, New York, N.Y.
10022

Carol Publishing Group books are available at special discounts
for bulk purchases, for sales promotions, fund raising, or
educational purposes. Special editions can be created to
specifications. For details contact: Special Sales Department,
Carol Publishing Group, 120 Enterprise Avenue, Secaucus, N.J.
07094

Manufactured in the United States of America

10 9 8 7 6 5 4 3 2 1

Library of Congress Cataloging–in–Publication Data

Offitzer, Karen.
    The Learning Annex guide to starting your own import/export
business / by Karen Offitzer.
        p. cm.
    "A Citadel Press book."
    ISBN 0–8065–1321–7
    1. Trading companies—Handbooks, manuals, etc. 2. Exports—
Handbooks, manuals, etc. 3. Imports—Handbooks, manuals, etc.
4. New business enterprises—Handbooks, manuals, etc. I. Learning
Annex (Firm) II. Title. III. Title: Import/export business.
HF1010.O34 1992
658.7'2—dc20   92–9795
                                                      CIP

Contents

Starting Your Own
Import/Export Business

1 | *Starting an Import/ Export Business*

Are you ready to start traveling around the world on tax-deductible dollars?

Do you like the idea of buying products at bargain prices? Building your own business with other people's money? Bringing goods into the United States and shipping goods out? All, while making a sizable profit?

Whether they're sapphires from Bangkok, computers to Haiti, folk art from Antigua—or anything you decide people will buy and sell—the exciting trend toward free trade and open market systems around the world is making international trade the hottest business opportunity of the 1990s.

Perhaps you're an entrepreneur who wants to get involved in the worldwide selling and buying market. Or you love to travel. Maybe you relish the idea of starting your own business, possibly only part-time at first, setting your own, flexible, working hours.

Would you enjoy being your own boss? Delving into foreign commerce? Creating a profitable business? If any of these ideas appeal to you, then you've chosen the perfect starting place for a first peek into the world of import/ export. This step-by-step guide will lead you through the import/export business in simple, easy-to-understand language, and will help you determine if this is the field for you.

What Is the Import/Export Business?

The import/export business, simply put, is moving products and services across national boundaries. When goods are brought in from another country or overseas territory, this is *importing*. When goods are sent to another country or overseas territory, this is *exporting*. How do you choose between importing or exporting for your own business? Many people start with one, say importing, and then find opportunities that lead them into exporting. In chapter 2, you will have a chance to weigh the pros and cons of each side of the business trade and see which one works best for you.

Importing and exporting involves buying and selling in different countries. When the goods or services offered by someone are exchanged for currency or the goods and services offered by someone else, and this exchange takes place across national boundaries, this is called *international trade*.

What Is International Trade?

International trade is the business of trading across national boundaries. In this age of global interplay, people all over the world see the products, luxuries, and lifestyles of people in other parts of the world, and then *want* them. It is not surprising that the business of trading products between countries is growing as fast as it is.

People have always found ways to obtain goods that were either not available locally or were cheaper and better-made elsewhere. And with movies and television gaining access to virtually everywhere around the globe, the opportunity for people to see and desire products not easily available in their own country is creating a marketing boon for importers and exporters.

In addition, people have always enjoyed the status of owning exotic products from foreign lands, simply for the novelty of exhibiting "something different." Both need and desire have created a market that is ripe for entrepreneurs. The vast changes in world economy are making this an ideal time to begin taking part in the exciting, enlightening, and profitable international trade.

What Opportunities Exist in the Import/ Export Business?

People are entering the import/export business for many different reasons. Some cite the *travel opportunities* that are available to those who have made this their business. Others state the *financial opportunities* as the reason they've chosen to pursue a career in international trade. And still others say that the *lifestyle opportunities*—being your own boss and creating your own hours—are the best reasons for becoming an importer or exporter.

Travel Opportunities

You may have started thinking about the import/export business on a trip abroad—perhaps you came across some beautiful handmade items and thought that surely there would be a market for them in boutiques back home. And that started you thinking about a whole range of countries you could visit, searching out products you've never seen in the States, and then bringing them back to sell. If you speak a foreign language, or are attuned to certain foreign cultures, chances are you've already made contacts in countries that have interesting products to sell.

While the business of importing and exporting items involves many other activities and skills—from purchasing and marketing, to administrative responsibilities—the ability to spot bargains while traveling is a definite asset. And, by keeping excellent records and documenting your business expenses while abroad, traveling can become a tax-deductible expense of international trade.

Financial Opportunities

Importers and exporters learn how to "buy" and "sell" goods without using their own money. One example is a "letter of credit" which is a document that guarantees payment in advance. By analyzing the profit margin available at different rates of purchasing and selling, you can figure out in advance how much money is to be made in any particular transaction. Another way of seeking financial success is by becoming an agent, representing companies or individuals in international transactions, with the company or individual footing the bill.

Many opportunities for financial success are available to the importer or exporter who:

- understands the market
- has the skills necessary to purchase and market products
- can administer and manage a multifaceted business

Lifestyle Opportunities

The advantages of being your own boss and running your own business are, to many, key reasons for pursuing an importing and exporting career. Those who are successful in the field have much to be envied for:

- flexible hours
- "paid" trips to foreign countries
- the opportunity to be involved in international politics and cultures
- the chance to practice a variety of skills on the job
- the diversity in each day's activities

It is not the lifestyle for everyone. If, however, you think you have the skills and flexibility to be happy in a business where every aspect will be, at times, both frustrating and challenging, then a life-style that involves these activities may be the right choice for you.

Who Is Getting Into the Business?

Everyone is getting into the business!

- Entrepreneurs
- People who want to work from home
- Couples who enjoy working and traveling together
- Businesses that have a product that they think would be useful overseas
- Those who want to start a business part-time while pursuing a career
- Just about anyone who enjoys business and has a taste for international trade!

Entrepreneurs who see the changing market and are aware of its possibilities in the trade business are seeking more information to increase their profits.

Individuals and couples who are looking for a venture to start that involves various skills and offers the opportunity for large profits are finding success in this business.

People who want to start slowly, choosing something that can be done part-time, while learning more about international trade, quotas, customs, business plans, and marketing and distribution, are finding the import/export business an exciting and profitable one.

Are you willing to:

- learn the "language" of the import/export business?
- study the market?
- organize a business plan?

- begin enjoying the particulars of international trade such as travel and foreign cultures?
- discover more about international economics?

If you answered yes to most of these questions, you are on your way toward becoming a successful importer/exporter.

When Is a Good Time to Start?

Once you decide on the particulars of your business you can begin working in international trade. Questions you'll need to answer include:

- whether to work full-time or part-time
- whether to import or export
- what you want to sell or buy
- how you will handle the financial and transportation transactions
- where you will market your products

A good time to start is as soon as you thoroughly understand the risks and gains, along with the specific terminology of the import/export business. Being prepared will help you move in the direction of success.

How Do I Get Started?

Chapter two will help you decide how you can best fit into the import/export business. Chapters three and four will aid in your understanding of the purchasing aspects of importing and exporting. Chapters five and six will deal with marketing. In chapter seven you'll learn the vocabulary of international trade, including regulations, transportation, and payment, answering the question "What do I need to know to conduct business across international borders?" And chapters eight and nine will discuss travel and administrative tasks which should help you begin planning trips and creating your own business. Finally, in chapter ten, you'll learn about the various government, public, and private sources which provide information that can substantially increase your knowledge and awareness of international trade.

How do you get started? Start thinking, start planning, start doing...and before long, you'll be participating, hopefully successfully, in the import/export business.

Summary

The import/export business is open to everyone—students, entrepreneurs, homemakers, salespeople, couples, and individuals. It can be pursued part-time or full-time, from a home or from an office, from New York City or from Lake Charles, Louisiana. Knowing the terminology, the risks involved, and the opportunities available in an import/export business can help you decide if this is the right choice for you.

Importing When goods are brought in from another country or overseas territory.

Exporting When goods are sent to another country or overseas territory.

International trade When the goods or services offered by someone are exchanged for currency or the goods and services offered by someone else, and this exchange takes place across national boundaries.

2 | *Are You Right for This Business?*

What makes some people successful in this business and others fail? Knowing what tasks are involved, and being able to assess your own particular skills and interests, are steps towards ensuring success. As in any enterprise, the import/export business requires several different elements. Certain decisions need to be reached before embarking on an importing or exporting venture. This chapter will discuss the major questions you need to ask yourself. You'll be introduced to the various tasks involved, from choosing where you'll be doing business to what kind of paperwork you can expect. Understanding the different choices you have is one step toward determining if this is the right business for you.

Import or Export?

Importing or exporting—which is easier? The answer depends on your knowledge of languages and cultures, and your ability to make dependable contacts both here and abroad. Buying, in general, is usually easier than selling. If the harder task of selling your goods is done in the country with which you're most familiar, chances are you'll find you're better able to test products, close deals, and change marketing strategies when needed. Thus, many people say importing, selling products on familiar territory, is easier.

One suggestion is to begin with either importing or exporting, but not both, and learn the specific transactions involved. It's easy enough to switch gears once you understand the process that takes place. While there are some differences in terms and regulations that you will need to know, the basic tenets of international trade are the same for importing and exporting. Once you understand one, you will have little trouble transferring your skills to the other.

Merchant or Agent?

Working as a merchant means you are performing all the import and export functions for your transaction; you buy the goods and try to sell them. Your risk and expenses will be higher, but so will your level of profitability. If you can afford to buy the goods you want to sell, you may want to work as a merchant. If you prefer selling to buying, you may want to work as an agent. An agent spends more time selling the products than buying them. As an agent, you are getting customers to buy a product that you are selling *for* someone else. While a formalized agreement with a supplier can protect you from risk, you will not have as much control over your business as you would as a merchant. Also, your profit potential may not be as high.

Full-Time or Part-Time?

Beginning the process of importing or exporting an item can be done on a part-time basis. Many individuals prefer learning the business as they go along, rather than jumping into it full-time. Dealing with foreign countries can be fun and exciting—even if you *don't* make a profit right away!

Part-time offers obvious advantages. You can keep your job and start learning the business slowly. You can begin experimenting with importing or exporting, small items or large, working as an agent or merchant. Of course the profit margin for a smaller, part-time operation will most likely be smaller, and you may find the time and effort it takes to keep on top of any single transaction is more than you can handle on an evening-and-weekend basis. Depending on what countries you are dealing with, you may need to be able to reach people during working hours, and those working hours may conflict with your own.

If you choose to start full-time, you will probably need to make a profit within a few months. This requires being exceptionally clear as to your risks, responsibilities, and potential profit margin before you begin.

Deciding whether to work full-time or part-time should depend on your resources, both financial and emotional, and your ability to handle many tasks at once. You may also want to consider how feasible it is to commit a certain number of hours a week to a part-time business—you don't want to start a transaction and then find you are unable to perform the numerous steps along the way.

What Should I Buy or Sell?

While this may seem like an easy question to answer for some of you—perhaps you're reading this book because you found a delicious candy bar in Spain and are anxious to begin selling it in the United States—you do need to understand the criteria for importing or exporting products. The first rule is to choose a product with which you are familiar. The product may need to be adapted for import into a certain country, or you may need to explain to buyers how it works or what it does. Perhaps you sense a continuing growth in computers and are hoping to export computer programs. Are you familiar enough with different hardware and software that may be available in foreign countries? Once you've chosen a product that you feel comfortable selling, you also need to test your product against these additional criteria:

- Is it easily available?
- Is it practical to transport this product?
- Is the market open to this type of product?
- Is this product legal to import or export?

In chapter 3 we will talk about how to find specific products and suppliers. Chapter 7 will discuss import and export regulations. There are many sources to go to if you have no idea what you want to buy or sell, only that you want to get involved in international trade. While having a product in mind may get you started, many people first find out how it's done, and then look for the product with which to do it. Both methods can be very successful.

Where Should I Buy or Sell?

As in choosing a product, the best rule of thumb is to begin with what you know. If you're fluent in Swedish and have friends or family in Sweden, who are eager to help, you have an excellent base. Many who start importing or exporting have visited a specific country several times, on business or for pleasure, and are aware of the local business and social customs. Knowing how individuals in foreign countries conduct business can put you at a distinct advantage when planning an international arrangement for products to be either bought or sold. Another import factor is learning what government regulations are required for items to be bought or sold abroad. Chapter 4 will help you not only select a market for your product but also understand the need for professional contacts and trustworthy sales representatives wherever you choose to do business.

What Will I Be Doing?

The related activities of importing or exporting fall into five categories:

- purchasing
- marketing
- international trade
- travel
- administration

You don't have to love every aspect of the business, but it certainly helps if you have an understanding of what you'll be doing on a regular basis as an importer/exporter. It also helps you discover what skills you need to brush up on before putting your time and money into international trade.

Purchasing

The act of buying products may be what intrigues you about the business. Perhaps you've seen exquisite sapphires in Bangkok and want to turn them into rings and bracelets to sell in the United States. Or maybe you like the idea of traveling to various countries, exploring local trade fairs and flea markets for unique crafts that just don't seem to be made anywhere in the States. Even if buying products isn't a favorite hobby, be aware that you will spend a lot of time on the following activities:

- carefully choosing a product
- checking quality
- figuring out how much you can pay and for what quantity
- planning how to best pack and ship your goods

The purchasing of products is an area that will take substantial research and time. Even though buying goods is relatively easy compared to trying to sell them, it is an area that takes well thought-out planning and careful selection.

Marketing

Are you aware of the number of places you can market and sell your goods? Importers sell:

- to department and retail stores
- through mail order companies
- through small boutiques
- through catalogs
- directly to homes, schools, and offices

And exporters sell items from the U.S. to foreign markets through many of the same venues. What you need to be able to offer these vendors is a better product, or a lower price, or excellent service, or perhaps longer credit. Understanding the market—knowing where to sell your product and how much to sell it for in order to maximize your profits is a large part of the import/export game. After selecting and buying your specific product, you need to be able to sell it to customers for your business to be successful—and marketing skills are key assets for successful importers and exporters.

International Trade

Knowing the economies and business practices of the countries you will be buying from or selling to are important aspects of the import/export business. If you already have an interest in foreign affairs, you are ahead of the game. Knowledge about the countries you are interested in can be easily gained, however, and there are many sources to help you. Chapter 7 will give specific guidelines, not only about what you need to know, but about how to obtain the necessary information.

Aspects of international trade that you will need to become familiar with include:

- quotas
- custom regulations
- foreign banks
- international documentation
- foreign monies
- international trade regulations

As an importer or exporter, knowing the applicable laws of the countries on both sides of the transaction will put you in the best possible position for making a successful deal. Every transaction will involve a certain amount of international red tape—it is best to figure out, up-front, what you need to know, and where to get the most up-to-date information.

Travel

Passports, visas, time changes, local currency, customs—while travel to exotic countries is, for many, one of the highlights of a career in the import/export business, it is time consuming and should be counted as one of the activities on which you will be spending time and money. The importance of traveling to the destination of your products, whether you are buying or selling them, will be discussed further in chapter 8. For purposes of "job description" however, the amount of travel and travel-related activity can be substantial and must be given a fair amount of research and planning.

Administration

How are you with bookkeeping and accounting? The amount of administrative work involved in each transaction depends on the specifics of your trade, but virtually no trade takes place without substantial time spent on administrative tasks. Starting your business will include:

- creating your business plan

- processing documentation
- keeping records
- preparing inventories
- maintaining financial records

As your business grows, so will your administrative responsibilities. If you are planning to enter the import/export business full-time, you may be thinking about an office. And what about a fax machine, or telex, or a computer, and a copier? In addition to being your own boss, you need to think about whether you also want to be your own accountant, bookkeeper, office manager, and secretary. Many people who succeed in importing or exporting have created a system of dealing with paperwork that stresses organization and maintenance. If you're one of those people who love statistics and forms, you certainly can count that as an asset in this business.

Summary

Starting any business takes a little bit of this, a little bit of that. It's the right combination of skills, interests, and desire that allows some people to create their little—or big—corner of wealth. Knowing what's involved is the first step toward deciding if you can do it, and for every area of expertise that you do have, there are books and courses and seminars to help you learn the things you don't. A successful importer or exporter can be a great traveler, a great bargain hunter, a great salesperson, or even a great bookkeeper—having the interest and willingness to learn the not-so-favorite skills are part of what makes every successful importer and exporter uniquely different.

Merchant   A buyer and seller of commodities for profit.

Agent   One who acts for, or in the place of another as, a representative.

3 | *Purchasing: What Will I Import?*

$\mathbf{F}$inding the right product can be as simple as stumbling across beautiful handmade puppets in Guatemala or can take a substantial amount of time and decision making. Some common questions arise:

- Should I first choose the country or the product I want to deal with?
- Do I look first to see what's available in the U.S. or do I assume I can sell any imported product if I find a quality item?
- Must I price my product lower than competitors?
- Do I need to travel abroad to find my product?
- Are there ways to find products without leaving the country—or even my own home?

Whether you already have a product in mind, or want to know how to find the best possible product to import for maximum income potential, this chapter can help you figure out:

- where to look
- how to find out if your "perfect idea" is feasible for the U.S. market
- what your options are
- how to get samples to show to potential customers

While there are government restrictions and quotas which

can apply to your product (see chapter 7 for information on restrictions), most items *can* be brought into the U.S. without a license or permit, making your choices virtually limitless.

Selecting Products

Which comes first—the country or the product? This decision may be easy if you're already fluent in a foreign language and enjoy traveling to a particular country. Several visits to Israel, for example, and the ability to speak the native tongue of the local craftspeople, may have given you ample ideas for handmade holiday products. Perhaps you found items you believe would eagerly be bought by U.S. customers for that added touch at religious celebrations. Many people start their import business with a product they've discovered on a trip—they bring back a few samples, show them to buyers, and, in some cases, are given immediate orders to fill. Others start with a product in mind and search for the best foreign supplier of that item. If you're background is in fashion design, for example, you may decide you want to import silk dresses. You'll then want to look for a way to find what countries produce these items, and who you can speak to about creating your designs to import. Whether you choose the country or the product first, there are many sources to turn to for help. Once you grasp the opportunities that are available, use the specific source information, discussed in chapter 10, for initiating contacts.

Choosing the Country

You're fluent in Spanish, love traveling to Spain, and want to find out what products you can import from that country. There are several sources that can provide information about what products are currently imported from a specific country, as well as what agencies exist to help you choose items from a particular area.

Trade Statistics

The U.S. Department of Commerce publishes a wealth of information for importers and exporters, including statistics on what products are being imported from the country in question. There are directories which serve as guides to the people, products, and marketing opportunities in the U.S. import industry, and guides to the requirements that an importer must meet to enter goods. Chapter 10 gives names and addresses of helpful sources.

Trade Promotion Offices

Novices to the import/export business are usually amazed at the number of organizations that exist to help bring products into the country. One source for helping you choose a product to import from a specific country is that country's trade promotion office in the United States. Most countries do have trade offices here, and many of them can be contacted by mail or phone. See chapter ten for additional information.

Foreign Countries' Export Promotion Offices

Just as the United States has offices to help people import and export, many foreign countries have their own organizations to promote exporting. These organizations can be very useful to individuals looking for products to import. An export promotion office in Taiwan, for example, will give a potential importer access to publications which describe what products are available for exportation.

Choosing the Product

Getting product ideas can be one of the more fun aspects of starting an import/export business, and is one area that you can begin working on immediately. Simply by subscribing to various trade publications, you can begin to receive information about products in various countries that foreign manufacturers and/or suppliers are eager to have you import into the United States. You can decide to choose your product by:

- visiting several countries and seeing what's available
- doing research at a local library
- attending trade shows and exhibitions
- selecting from catalogs in the comfort of your home

The options for how to find products to import are almost as varied as the products themselves. Addresses and listings for specific publications and information sources are covered in the final chapter.

Trade Publications

Are you aware of the number of publications that advertise products, available for importing, from all over the world? There are newspapers, magazines, and brochures that specifically cover:

- certain areas (a series of publications called *Made in Europe*, for example)
- certain types of products (*Asian Sources* has a separate magazine for electronics, or computers, or toys)
- items for specific professions (one of *Made in Europe*'s publications is called *Medical Equipment*)

Many of these publications consist solely of advertisements for products from just about everywhere, and list addresses and contact numbers for more information. Some publications also list importing opportunities, which usually are requests from specific manufacturers or suppliers for individuals to initiate an export/import trade exclusively for them.

Trade Shows and Exhibits

If looking at the real thing seems an easier, more precise way to choose a product than sifting through catalogs, you can attend trade shows and exhibitions to find the product you want to import. There are international directories which provide information about scheduled events such as fairs and festivals, trade and industrial shows, merchandise marts and expositions. All this information can be accessed through most libraries or through the publications listed in chapter ten. Most major industries have trade shows to advertise and promote their international trade, and this is a chance for you to discover foreign products without traveling the world to do so.

Traveling to Find Your Products

Once you've chosen a country or a product to pursue for import ideas, it is important to strongly consider traveling to wherever you'll be doing business before embarking on major financial deals. It always helps to see in person the people with whom you are dealing, and you can often meet directly with manufacturers, or export industry personnel. This can help make your decision a more informed and, therefore, more enlightened one. You'll want to be wary of items you've discovered through publications and not find people at the other end willing to deal with you—it's important, no matter what choices you make, to feel comfortable with the supplier, or manufacturer, of any particular product.

Finding Suppliers

Many of the sources for finding products will lead you to suppliers, but it helps if you know the difference between suppliers who are manufacturers and those who are export trading companies. The more information you have, the better position you'll be in to find the best person or company for your importing transaction. It is more desirable to import from manufacturers than from export trading companies, since you will then have direct contact with the outfit making the goods. When you visit, you will be able to see the factories, personnel, and equipment supporting your import business. This may be difficult, however, if you are dealing in very small quantities. In such cases, using an export trading company that is dealing with several manufacturers and buyers and can better afford to process small orders, might be the smarter option. Some choices for picking suppliers may be made for you, if you select a country to deal with, such as Japan, that relies predominantly on export trading companies. Other options available for you include:

- setting up your own advertisement
- contacting an international bank
- getting in touch with export promotion agencies in foreign countries

Researching both the country and the product that you choose will help you decide which type of supplier is best for you.

Advertising

You can put your own advertisement in the same publications that foreign suppliers are using to find importers. Letting manufacturers know that you are interested in buying their product and selling it in the United States is one way of finding a supplier who is interested in working with you.

International Banks

Since many banks work closely with importers and exporters to arrange financing and payment for their customers, they have access to many foreign suppliers and manufacturers. You can contact banks that advertise their services for individuals or companies involved in international trade, and see if they can provide you with helpful information.

Export Promotion Agencies

If you are visiting a country and are interested in buying some products, whom should you contact? You may want to speak with officials of that country's trade organizations. Another good choice is the local chamber of commerce, or any other organizations in that country that promote trade with the United States. It helps to visit potential suppliers and see for yourself if they have the capability of manufacturing and delivering the goods across international borders.

Industry Publications

You may be starting to realize that there are lists, books, magazines, and government sources for most of the information you need. Manufacturers and suppliers are no exception. Every industry publishes lists of manufacturers, and libraries generally will have access to these directories. There are even sources you can access with a computer and a modem. Looking for toothbrush manufacturers? Try the *Encyclopedia of Business Information Sources* to find out what guides are available in that industry. You may spend lots of times looking up lists to find other lists, but once you realize that you have massive amounts of necessary information available at your fingertips, you'll probably wonder why you didn't start this process sooner.

Getting Samples

Have you ever ordered something from a mail order catalog only to find, upon receipt of that item, that it was too big, too small, too cheap-looking, or just too plain ugly for you to want anymore? Pictures in catalogs often mask qualities that an object actually has, or doesn't have. Pictures rarely provide an adequate representation of the product's color or texture. So should you order ten thousand pieces of "Harry, The Flower Growing Frog" from a foreign catalog without checking to make sure that Harry does, indeed, grow flowers? If you answered no, chances are you're already thinking about getting a sample "Harry" first, and checking it out. In addition to finding out if the product looks, feels, and acts like it's supposed to, you will also probably need samples to show to potential buyers. Having the product in hand will also help you figure out:

- if it needs to be adapted for a particular market
- if it is a quality item
- if it traveled well
- if it meets U.S. standards (more about that in chapter 7)

Free Samples

Once you're selected a product or a group of products that you may be interested in importing, you need to contact the manufacturer or supplier and ask for samples. Will they send you free ones? Some will, but it's probably best to offer to pay—they may send them to you free, anyway, but it won't look like you're trying to get something for nothing. Don't be scared off by minimum orders required in advertisements. A letter stating that you may be interested in importing their product and that you would like a sample, or that you need a specified amount for test marketing, is usually honored.

Paying for Samples

If you want to save time and be a little more certain that you'll receive the samples, you may want to send payment with your request. A good rule of thumb, if you're requesting a product through an advertisement that lists prices, is to send the amount listed as their lowest price (regardless of how few you are requesting), and add the approximate cost of insured air mail. You can get an international money order from a commercial bank, and can send it along with a letter requesting samples of the product for possible importing.

Adapting Products for the Market

In choosing a product, from any source, you should be aware of how it will work in the U.S. market. Aside from government regulations barring certain products and requiring specific restrictions for others (see chapter 7), you need to be aware of customer preferences, product standards, and any technical specifications that may apply.

Product Standards

Although many standards regarding flammability, safety, food and drug laws, and pollution controls for foreign countries may be similar or even parallel to those of the United States, you must be aware of any differences before selling foreign products in the U.S. market. Checking legal requirements with a customs office, including labeling and packaging requirements, will help you decide if importing your specific product is feasible.

Technical Specifications

Does your product need to be plugged in electrically? Check the voltage of any electrical product you're thinking of importing—if you've traveled, no doubt you're aware of the frustration of plugging in your hair dryer or electric razor, only to find out that while the U.S. uses 120V, 60hz, much of the world uses 220V, 50hz. While carrying an adaptor is fine for traveling, you may want to see if the product you're planning to import can be made for use with U.S. specifications. Also check to see what system of weights and measures is used on those ornately-designed measuring cups you found in Norway—while the United States still primarily uses pounds and ounces, the metric system is the predominant choice in the rest of the world.

Summary

Choosing the right product is one of the most important steps in creating a successful import business. Knowing where to look, what to look for, what restrictions may affect your choice, and what standards are required, will put you ahead of the game when selecting your product.

Department of Commerce The agency of government whose purpose it is to promote commercial industrial interests in the country.

Customs The procedures and organization involved in the collection of duties levied by a country on imports and exports.

License or permit A permission granted by government authority to engage in an import or export business.

4 | *Purchasing: What Will I Export?*

Many of the guidelines for choosing products to bring into the country apply to exporting products as well. Understanding your product, making contacts, and knowing what the legal and marketing requirements are for the country you choose to export to, are all keys to finding a product that can help your business become successful. Whether you're an established tennis teacher who wants try exporting instructional videos, a furniture painter who wants to export painting equipment, or anyone who wants to take advantage of the customers overseas, your exporting success can greatly depend upon:

- how well you adapt your product to the needs and wants of the foreign markets
- how much research you've done into the import regulations of foreign countries
- what, currently, is being successfully exported

Product or Country?

As in importing, you need to decide if you want to first find a product and then decide which country (or countries) to export to, or if you want to choose a country that interests you and then investigate what kind of consumer demand you can fill there. There are ways to identify markets for

your chosen product, or products for your chosen market—
both avenues are open for your business.

Product

Let's say you're an avid golf player and believe that this
great sport must be catching on in other countries. You have
a few contacts with golf club manufacturers and want to see
if equipment might make a good exporting venture. How
can you find out? And, once you do, how will you learn if
other companies from the United States are already exporting golf equipment? One way to start would be to check
international trade statistics (as described in chapter 3) and
find out what kind of export activity is already being done to
various countries. Another way is to talk to other golf
players who may have done some traveling, and ask them if
they've noticed the sport being played elsewhere. Golf pros
at clubs may be able to add some information, and organizations which sponsor tournaments may be able to tell you
where their best players are coming from. By zeroing in on
foreign markets, researching trade statistics, and talking
with individuals familiar with the countries you've identified, you have begun the process of choosing a product that
can be a successful export item.

Country

Perhaps you're more interested in filling needs of specific
countries. You enjoy the prospect of finding the best deal in
the United States to supply the needs of foreign markets.
How do you find what those needs are? Some steps you can
take are:

- checking with publications and newsletters that list
  products needed overseas
- advertising in foreign publications
- traveling to the countries of your choice and seeing
  what product void there is that you can fill

Once you have information about what item might be needed abroad, you can begin looking for a supplier, in the United States, and start the process of exploring the various costs involved—buying, packing, shipping, administration—to see if the product is profitable to export.

Finding Suppliers

Whether your selection of product comes from choosing the needs of a particular country or from the research into what countries could use the product you have in mind, you need to line up U.S. suppliers who are willing and able to export their product for foreign markets.

Publications

Almost every industry in the United States has its own trade magazine or newsletter. Accessing these publications is an excellent way to choose potential suppliers for whatever product you have in mind. One comprehensive directory, the *Thomas Register of American Manufacturers*, is generally available in libraries. It lists addresses, locations, and telephone numbers of manufacturers of virtually every product imaginable.

Government Support

The United States government supports exporting through the International Trade Administration, part of the Department of Commerce. There is an organization called the Foreign Commercial Service, which provides investment and financial counseling to individuals and businesses. Many publications are available by mail, or from government bookstores (see chapter 10 for location information).

Adapting Products

Be sure to check government regulations for the country you want to deal with to see if any restrictions apply to the product you have in mind. Again, as with importing, be sure to check product standards (flammability, safety, food and drug laws, and pollution controls) and technical specifications (weights and measures, voltage, etc.) before arranging an exporting deal. Keep in mind that even very large firms have had trouble introducing products in foreign markets. Be sure that you understand the market and the customers you are dealing with before spending large amounts of money on exporting any product that is new and/or different.

Special Concerns

Suppose you've followed through with a company in Panama which requested fishing poles. You've lined up a U.S. manufacturer willing to export, made the financial and transportation arrangements, and sent a large number of fishing poles to the company. Sometime after the products arrive in Panama, you are contacted by the company and told that customers are returning the product—the fishing poles break when a fish pulls on them! Since you are the Panama company's only contact, it wants to know what you will do. So, what will you do? Warranties and service contracts, servicing arrangements and responsibility are all details you will need to arrange beforehand to keep situations like this from putting an end to your venture. Remember that U.S. warranties are not necessarily international. You must verify, in writing, what will be expected of you as the agent between the manufacturer and the foreign importer.

Summary

An exporting business may be more difficult to start from scratch than an importing one, but that doesn't mean it's less profitable. Knowing your product and being able to sell it are key elements whether you're importing or exporting.

Becoming aware of the special concerns involved in exporting items is important in helping you decide which side of the business—importing or exporting—will be the most fulfilling, and profitable, for you. If you are familiar with the needs of a particular country and can make arrangements with a distributor in that country, finding a manufacturer in the United States is a relatively easy task, and this can be your entry into the import/export business.

5 | *Marketing: Where Do I Sell My Imports?*

You've chosen your product, shown it around to a few possible consumers to see how it will fare in the U.S. market, and carefully selected a foreign supplier willing to work with you. Now you're ready to move along to the next step in your import transaction—actively marketing your product in the United States. This chapter will cover:

- ways to get into the domestic market, (especially on a limited budget)
- what you should know about marketing to build a successful business
- what you need to do to get started

Finding Customers

How do you find customers for your product? How about walking into your favorite store, talking to the buyer, convincing him or her to order some of your products,and then putting your deal in writing? This *is* one way of marketing your product, but it may not be the most profitable or feasible for your particular product. Perhaps you have an industrial product, such as computer keyboards for businesses, or laundry folding machines for hospitals. Or you want to sell your product directly to consumers, but think it would work best through large chains, and the buyers are several hundred miles away. Another situation to consider is how to start the marketing process when you have a very specialized product—brass piano lamps from Brussels, for example—and want to reach piano aficionados worldwide. By first understanding the different choices you have in selling and marketing your product, you can better evaluate the different strategies.

Industrial Products

If you have selected an item that you think will work best for industry use (in a factory, an office, a hospital, for example), you may want to look into selling directly for that purpose or to industrial distributors. Or perhaps you've found an item to import that can be used for another product, such as shoelaces, that can be sold directly to manufacturers of shoes, for example. Or you could contact shoe repair shops, or manufacturers of other shoe items, and see if they import similar ones and would be willing to bring in yours (for a better price or better service, or because they're better-made laces, etc.). If you found a fascinating array of handmade buttons in a small foreign village, perhaps you could import directly to clothing manufacturers or companies that produce sewing kits.

Consumer Products

Many products that are imported are sold directly to consumers. If your intended product is meant to be used in the home, this is a consumer good. While the same product can be a consumer good or an industrial good (buttons bought by clothing manufacturers are industrial goods, while loose buttons bought by a customer for home sewing are consumer goods), it's important to think about the possible choices you have in finding the right market for your product. You can be importing to both industrial and consumer markets at the same time, depending on whom you are choosing as the buyer.

Marketing as an Agent or Merchant

Remember the distinctions outlined in chapter two? If you're working as a merchant, you are performing all the import and export functions for your transactions: purchasing the goods, bringing them to the United States, and supplying them to your buyers. As an agent, you are representing the product to buyers, and acting as a middleman to conclude a transaction between the domestic importer and the foreign exporter.

Selling Your Product as an Agent

Perhaps you found a wonderful mapmaker in Greece and want to arrange for his or her exquisite handmade works to be bought by museums and art galleries in the United States. You identified these stores through phone directories in several large cities, and you know that art dealers, who often transport artwork by air mail, will most likely be able to perform the actual import functions. You're not concerned with the actual customers of the maps; you feel that the art dealers will take care of that. As the representative for the mapmaker, you have a formal agreement that says you will be the sole contact in the United States for the maps. Any art stores or museum shops that want to purchase these maps must do so through you. In this instance, you have become an import agent. Other approaches to keep in mind, when working as an agent, are identifying possible companies that already import products similar to yours, or companies that manufacture like products. The sources chapter at the end of this book provides some listings for gathering this information. Once you establish yourself as an agent, you will be representing imported items to a domestic market, obtaining orders, and giving these orders to your overseas supplier. They will handle the shipping and payment of the product; as an agent, you will receive your fee (generally called a commission) from the supplier.

Selling Your Product as a Merchant

As a merchant you will not receive a commission, or fee, from the supplier. Your money will come in the form of direct payment from the buyer. If you arrange to pay for and import handcarved pencils for Antigua, you then need to get payment directly from any buyer—a stationery store, for instance—that you've interested in this product. The amount of money you receive will hopefully cover the expense of the product itself along with the shipping and handling fees you've already paid. In order for you to make a profit, of course, the amount you receive should be more than your actual costs. You don't always need to put all the money up front for the products and this will allow you some protection from having 10,000 handcarved pencils piled high in your living room with no one willing to buy them. It's generally a better idea to order samples and get bona fide offers before ordering large shipments. While the profit to be made selling as a merchant—performing all the import and export functions yourself—will more likely be higher than if you're working as an agent, it's important to be aware of the risks involved in putting the money up front for any overseas transaction.

Where to Market Your Product

There are several options for you as either an agent or a merchant, whether you're importing goods for industrial or consumer use. As with any marketing strategy, some will work for certain products and not with others. Your most profitable choice of product will probably depend on the following factors:

- type
- transportability
- relative quality of your product
- appropriateness in certain types of markets
- photogenic qualities

These factors can all play a part in what choice you make in marketing your imports. If you're planning to sell your item at outdoor flea markets, for example, you need to be sure it can stand up to the heat/cold of the outdoors. If you think you can reach the most customers through a mail order catalog, you need to be sure that the picture of your item is, indeed, worth a thousand words, since you may not have space for more than a dozen well-chosen words to help sell it. Seeking the obvious and, more importantly, the not-so-obvious conditions of each of the available markets and the impact of your particular product in these markets may be the key toward making it stand out from the rest. This could mean the difference between success and failure. Some of the more common methods for selling your product include trade shows, sales representatives, mail order, department stores, boutiques, flea markets, swap meets, and street vendors. Each has specific requirements which may work well with your product; none is necessarily better than others for all products.

Trade Shows

Attending international trade shows can be an effective way to make contacts and learn about potential customers, distributors, markets, products, and your competition. Trade shows include industrial shows and expositions, and you can usually find listings of these events at your local library. Chapter 10 includes additional sources. For the beginning importer (or exporter), trade shows can be a real eye-opener, letting you see the different kinds of products that are imported, and simply getting you involved in the process of learning about the market. You can often get literature and samples of products at these shows, and can get an overall picture of what is happening in the import business. You'll also see what kinds of products are being bought and sold, and who is doing the buying and selling. You also can exhibit your own product at a trade show, in order to find customers and distributors.

Sales Representative

How about putting an ad in one of the trade directories that circulate at these shows looking for representatives to sell your imported item? There are independent salespeople who would love to hook up with importers needing to place their product. If you can provide samples or perhaps catalogs of your product to salespeople who, in turn, will try to get orders for you, this may be a way for you to market your product.

Mail Order

The mail order business is a popular and growing one in its own right. Understanding how it works is vital to anyone who is trying to sell a product through this means. For importers, selling through mail order has added concerns. Besides learning about the various elements of mail order, you need to take into account the risks of advertising a product that is shipped from overseas—the time delays, quality control, and additional regulations and expenses involved in international transactions. Does this mean mail order is not a good idea for importers? On the contrary—an "exotic" item, or simply an item that is unavailable domestically, can be an excellent choice for mail order. While gaining a more thorough understanding of the mail order business would be in order before you begin selling through this means, we will discuss a few of the more popular methods available to you.

MAILING LISTS. There are companies that will allow you to rent or buy their mailing lists. Doing some research on what kind of customer is appropriate for your product, and then what mailing lists are available that reach those customers, is one way of getting an advertisement of your product into the homes of carefully selected, potential customers. You can also find companies that prepare your mailing, from designing and printing your advertisement, to stuffing, addressing, and stamping your envelopes. Of course, the fee for this service is an expense you need to take into account before choosing this option, and many importers with a single item to sell may find the cost prohibitive. You're up against expensive, glossy, multipage catalogs that also reach people in their homes. A single page advertisement may not solicit enough orders for this to be a worthwhile investment.

MAIL ORDER CATALOGS. If you can identify a mail order company that sells products similar to yours, you can try getting your product advertised in their catalog. In addition to collecting catalogs, you can find publications that will provide names and addresses of mail order companies. Most likely you will need to work through that company's buyer and to show proof that you have enough quantity in stock to fulfill all orders the company receives. This and other mail order options should be explored fully before spending the up-front money for large stock and expensive advertising.

ADVERTISING IN MAGAZINES AND NEWSPAPERS. Look through special interest magazines. See which ones show products that are similar to yours. An imported porcelain flower vase, for example, may be of interest to readers of housekeeping magazines, or home decorating magazines, or gardening magazines. If your imported product is hair accessories from Spain, check out magazines for fashion, hair design, or accessories. See what ads are already being offered, and use that as a guideline for preparing your own advertisement. Your best bet for this kind of marketing strategy may be a very specialized product that you can advertise in a very specialized magazine. This may work for something like manuscript boxes for a writer's magazine, or personalized flight jackets in one geared specifically to pilots.

Department Stores

Most department stores and chain stores have buyers who are highly specialized. While a small store may have someone who buys "picture frames," at a department store you may need to choose among the buyer who handles "Silver Items," "Hand-Crafted Items," "Houseware Accessories," or perhaps "Bridal Gifts." As a vendor, you need to find out the buyer for your particular product and how to reach him or her. Ask questions. Find out if there are best days to call. Some vendors will see you by appointment only, and some advertise "open buying days" when you don't need an appointment. Arriving with an excellent sales presentation—complete with competitive pricing, a quality product, and well-researched product information—can help you get your foot in the door.

Boutiques

Small, specialty shops may be the right choice for your product. Once you've selected a number of likely shops where you feel your product will sell well, make appointments with their buyers. Bring samples with you. Establish a personal relationship with the buyer, and try to get him or her to place orders. While a high profit business may require more orders than a small specialty shop can offer, this may be a way for you to begin making money. It can also serve as a way for you to build a reputation as an honest vendor.

Swap Meets, Flea Markets, and Street Vendors

Selling at street fairs, flea markets, and weekend festivals is more than just a fun way to do some selling out of doors—it's an opportunity to capitalize on events that draw crowds in the hundreds of thousands. These are folks who enjoy shopping outdoors, bargaining for their purchases, and viewing hard-to-find, unique items. And imported items are often suitable, and profitable, ones for this kind of market. The "business" of flea markets, from how to pick the best locations to how to display your wares, is the subject of a growing number of seminars and publications. And within this business is a growing number of wholesalers who provide to flea market dealers. It's definitely a market with which you should become more familiar if your product is one you think may sell well in this kind of environment. Wholesalers who sell to flea market vendors often have contacts with buyers who sell at related markets such as street vendors and swap meets. See chapter 10 for publications that discuss the flea market business.

Pricing

What are your profit-related goals? Do you want your business to support your travel to exotic countries? Are you looking to make a small, part-time salary? Do you intend to make this a full-time, self-supporting business? These decisions will affect your pricing strategy, as will the particular characteristics of your product, the economy, and your marketing strategies. Study the market. See what your competitors are charging. Figure out the costs of purchasing, shipping, and other business-related expenses. Identifying these expenses will help you decide how to price your product to reach your personal and business goals.

Summary

While this chapter is at best a mini-survey of some of the elements of marketing, your importing success will greatly improve if you follow up on the areas with which you are least familiar. You may need to learn more about choosing a market, establishing a price, creating a sales presentation, or initiating contacts. Knowing the variety of options available to you enables you to match your product to the best possible market. This chapter is only a beginning to the learning you can do—seminars, courses, and books are available to give you additional information. Before you begin buying and selling, brush up on marketing techniques, creating a business plan, exploring the mail order business, selling at flea markets, and a wide range of other topics briefly mentioned in this chapter.

Industrial products   Goods that are used in industry.

Consumer products   Goods that directly satisfy human wants.

Sales representative   A representative who acts as a salesman, usually for a commission.

Commission   A fee paid to an agent for transacting a piece of business or performing a service (usually a percentage of the money received from a total paid to the agent responsible for the business).

6 | *Marketing: Where Do I Sell My Exports?*

Suppose you've chosen tennis rackets as the item you'd like to begin exporting. You are friendly with the vice president of a domestic tennis racket manufacturing firm, and have gotten a tentative commitment from his company to look into exporting arrangements. You have several friends from all over the world who say tennis is a growing, international sport. Finally, you are an avid tennis player who feels comfortable extolling the virtues of this sport and its equipment. You're off to a great start, but now you need to know:

- where to begin looking for international customers
- how to choose what country or countries to contact
- where to go for information
- from whom you need help, both domestically and abroad
- how to find them
- who will sell your goods at foreign markets
- what restrictions exist in your chosen country

Choosing the market for your exports involves making decisions about these areas and more. In this chapter we'll address the issues you need to consider and discuss what kind of help is available. Finding the right market for your export business is as essential to being successful as choosing the right product and creating the most profitable export procedures.

Finding the Market

When looking for potential customers for your exporting venture, you need to consider several characteristics of the product you've chosen as well as those of the markets you wish to explore. Only when you find a reasonably good match between what you're offering and the markets' needs, should you begin seeking contacts within those countries for possible export deals. Without doing the proper research, you could find yourself:

- exporting dog collars to countries that overwhelmingly prefer cats as pets
- selling car seats to a population that depends predominantly on bicycles for transportation
- exporting cigarette holders to countries where smoking is restricted and/or declining steadily
- selling baseball bats to countries that much prefer soccer

Choosing the Country

What factors should you consider when choosing the country? What makes some countries better for exporting to than others? The more information you gather about your potential choices, the better prepared you will be to decide on what markets to pursue. Some factors you want to research include the size of that country, its population, sources of income, currency, language, tariffs, and quotas. These are only some of the market indicators you need to explore. Keep in mind that things like climate, national sports, leisure time, etc. are all factors which can affect your product.

Size

Knowing both the size of a country's population and whether the country is primarily urban or rural are important factors for many export items. If the country is mainly urban, you can find different avenues for advertising and promotion than if it is mostly rural. The population demographics—age, male/female ratio, ethnic and religious majorities—all may affect your particular product. Should you begin exporting infant clothing to a population with an extremely low birth rate? Would hearing aids have a greater chance of success in a country with a high number of elderly citizens? Knowing the statistics of a population can help you decide if you're in the right ballpark for finding customers.

Sources of Income

How do people make money in the country you've chosen? What is the overall employment picture? How much do people earn on average? Do farmers make up a high percentage of the population? What about factory workers? Office workers? Is a large enough number of the population involved in the computer industry, for example, to warrant exporting computer dust covers? If the product you've chosen is management training videos, are you better off exporting to countries that have a growing track record for private businesses, or those that have government training requirements? The answer to this particular question may be tricky; some governments may be excellent customers of management training videos as they pride themselves on developing and training employees in their country. However, you may find English speaking countries with growing numbers of private businesses that are looking for ways to teach their employees the management techniques that U.S. companies have used to prosper. What about exporting coffee makers? Would it help to know if coffee was grown domestically in that country. If not, is coffee a large import? Again, the more research you do, the better choice you can make.

Currency

Other than knowing what currency you're dealing with and how it translates domestically, is it important to use the currency element of a foreign country to determine its likelihood as a market? The answer is a resounding yes, especially, if you're exporting to a country that is somewhat unfamiliar to you. For example, what if you decided to export small coin purses—only to realize, weeks into the process, that the country you've chosen uses predominately paper currency? Or, if coins are prevalent, what if you decided to export coin dispensers such as the ones ice cream vendors often use? Would you need to know the sizes of that country's coins—and if they would even fit into U.S.-made dispensers? And how do the denominations and use of the coins differ from domestic ones? Would "Penny loafers" export well to countries that don't use pennies?

Language

As long as you can communicate with specific represent-atives for purposes of transactions, is there any other language barrier which may affect exporting? As with currency, there may be other important factors to consider. It may be vital to know not only the dominant language, but what, if any, are the secondary ones in use in that country. You may do very well exporting English-language textbooks to countries that encourage English as a second language; on the other hand, there may be no market at all for your books if English is rarely used. Another point to consider: Can you export items that have English sayings on them? You may find T-shirts or coffee mugs with English words to be a popular item in foreign countries, but you should know how the words translate in the native languages. Knowing the language has important ramifications for more than just business transactions; being able to understand the local advertising and promotional tactics used by successful companies in that country can help you build a better export business.

Tariffs and Quotas

The legal restrictions for importing items in foreign countries are varied; what may be fine for one country may be illegal for its neighbor. Details of specifications, such as those discussed in chapters 3 and 4, should be given attention when deciding upon a country. Most countries have health and safety laws, and these laws may vary greatly from domestic requirements. Foreign government laboratories usually test pharmaceuticals, for example, even if they satisfy all U.S. standards. Once you've identified possible foreign markets, check to see if your product can be legally imported by that country. (See chapter 10 for where to get that information.) Even if you've discovered a potential market for your item while traveling in that country, and you've talked to several buyers who assure you of your products' legality, you should check with government sources and investigate all areas of possible concern. Otherwise you could spend a lot of time and money preparing an order, only to find it stuck in a foreign port for not adhering to a variety of import regulations.

Making Contacts

Once you've chosen the best market for your export, you probably want to find people in that country who will assist sales of your product. This may include finding agents or importers in each country, or finding sales reps or distributors. You will want to decide if you should sell to end-users, direct customers, through mail-order, or through foreign import agents to wholesalers or retailers. Some options to consider for choosing representatives in foreign countries include trade exhibits, lists of local distributors and agents, and travel.

Trade Exhibits

There are several trade exhibits overseas, and American exporters can participate in several ways. Finding when and where these shows are is easy; lists can be obtained from the U.S. Department of Commerce and the U.S. Chamber of Commerce, as well as industry associations and journals. In many instances, you send along product catalogs, brochures, videos, and other sales aids to be displayed at shows organized by embassies and consultants. The Department of Commerce and some state and local governments offer assistance to individuals who want to participate. These sources may help you find potential agents or distributors.

Foreign Distributors

Identifying distributors can be done through various directories. The U.S. Department of Commerce has lists of foreign traders, and there are several other sources which identify retailers, wholesalers, and industrial distributors. Direct contact with foreign organizations which will import your product may not be the easiest method for finding an importer, however. You may want to consider contracting with an agent, someone who will locate companies to import your product and work for you (for a commission) in getting sales and pushing your product. The U.S. Department of Commerce can help you find foreign representatives. You can also locate them through trade exhibits and through direct advertising in international trade publications.

Travel

As in choosing a product, sometimes the best method for deciding where to sell your exports and finding who can help you sell them, is by traveling to that country and doing some "on site" investigation. You can contact the local chambers of commerce, or various people in the industry, who can help you find distributors, retailers, or agents. If you've ever hired people for any job, you already know how important it can be to meet an individual and consider his or her characteristics based on factors other than words. This can help you get a better feeling for what kind of salesperson, or representative, he or she will make for your business.

Summary

There are several sources available for answers to the marketing questions posed in this chapter. Market indicators are the subject of elaborate marketing seminars and books, and the factors mentioned here are simply the beginning of an effective marketing plan for your exports. As long as you do your homework you can be pretty sure of avoiding obvious marketing blunders. Though no method is foolproof—market tastes can never be perfectly predicted—proper preparation will help you approach your business with information, insight, and a greater opportunity for making intelligent decisions.

Demographics   The statistical characteristics of populations (such as age and income) used to identify markets.

Currency   The medium of exchange, or barter.

Market indicators   Any of a group of statistical values that taken together give an indication of the market.

Tariffs   Duties imposed by a government on goods imported or exported.

Quotas   The amount (quantity) of a product which may be imported into a country without restrictions or penalties.

Foreign sales agent representative   One who serves as the foreign representative of a domestic supplier and tries to obtain sales abroad for that supplier.

Export merchant   One who sells directly to a foreign purchaser (not using a middleperson).

7 | *International Trade: What Do I Need to Know to Conduct Business Across International Borders?*

Part of the excitement and challenge of international trade is learning about government restrictions, custom requirements, quotas, trade acts, and international regulations. Every country has rules designed to protect the economy and security as well as the health and safety of its citizens, and with global changes in such areas as economics, environment, and the advances in technology, the regulations that exist to protect individuals and countries are constantly changing. Keeping up with international events is a prime factor to consider when building a successful import/export business. By knowing the effects on business of international affairs today, you can prepare for the implications of the events of tomorrow. This chapter will introduce you to:

- the government regulations that affect importing and exporting
- what you need to know to transport your goods to and from different countries
- how people in the import/export business deal with

sending and receiving payment for international transactions

Government Regulations

If you're thinking of importing an item from a foreign country, you need to know if the United States allows that item to be brought in, and also if the country of origin allows that item to be exported. Likewise, for exporting, you need to find out if the United States allows that item to be sent out, and if the country with which you're planning to do business is indeed allowed to import that product. How do you get this information? Several agencies of both the United States and foreign governments will provide you with information necessary for importing and exporting. There are publications available to you which outline the requirements you must meet to complete a legal import/export transaction.

Importing

To import into the United States, you need to be familiar with customs procedures, tariffs, quotas, entry documents, and import regulations. You also must find out if you need a license to import the items you have chosen, and, if so, how to obtain that license. While the information included here will help you understand terms and conditions of importing, the agency with which you need to be in touch for the necessary information regarding your particular importing situation (product and country) is the U.S. Customs Service office. (See chapter 10 for contact information.)

Licensing

As far as licensing is concerned, importing is generally easier than exporting. Most countries require importers to have a license before bringing in foreign goods. The United

States, however, allows importers to bring most items in without a license or permit. You still must check with customs to see if your item is restricted or banned, but, in general, the red tape connected to licensing is kept to a minimum. However, the person or business you are importing from, the foreign exporter, will most likely need a license from his or her country to export that item. This is so a government can protect its resources and control what is leaving its country. When in doubt as to whether your supplier is permitted to send you the item you plan to import, check with that country's consulate.

Customs

The customs office is your right arm when it comes to determining what changes you need to make, if any, in order for your chosen product to be legal to import. It provides a service (through *Classification and Value* officers—C & V officers) whereby you describe your product to the customs officer and you are told what "TSUS" (Tariff Schedule of the United States) number is on the product, how the product needs to be marked or labeled, and what the duty on that product is. "TSUS" is a listing of imported products with code numbers and descriptions. The number, or classification, assigned to your product helps determine the rate of duty. Virtually all imported products have code numbers and descriptions, and yours will probably fall under a specific category which has a specific rate of duty and will have specific labeling requirements. Be as prepared as possible before contacting customs. You should know as much as you can about your product—size, material(s), amounts of each, separate parts, etc. Since many products are made up of several components, for the most accurate information you may want to visit a C & V officer to show your product in person. This will minimize the possibility of any surprises in customs procedures regarding restrictions or qualifications for importing. Other information you should be sure to ask about are specific requirements for your product such as warnings, or laundering instructions, and whether any other federal laws are applicable. Be sure to inquire as to whom else you should consult about your product (for state and local laws) and if there is anything else you need to know.

Import Regulations

Although the customs office may not require a license for most goods, some merchandise is prohibited or restricted by other federal agencies. If your product falls into certain categories, you need to check with the agency that governs the import of that type of product to find out if it legally can enter the United States. The importing of agricultural commodities, for example, such as animals, animal foods, insects, plants, and poultry products, is regulated by the U.S. Food and Drug Administration (USFDA) and the Department of Agriculture (USDA). Household appliances, like refrigerators, dishwashers, and television sets, are subject to safety and energy laws regulated by the Consumers Products Effectiveness Branch of the Department of Energy. If you're planning to import wool-lined slippers from Pakistan, you need to check the Wool Products Labeling Act from the Federal Trade Commission (FTC) before trying to bring them in. And if your wool slipper distributor wants to sell you matching pajamas, find out what regulations are enforced by the Consumer Products Safety Commission to see if those products will meet flammability and other safety requirements. There are many regulatory bodies that govern imports of products, and you should check with the U. S. Customs Service for what agencies to contact for information about your particular item.

Labeling

The specific labeling or marking procedures required will probably include *country of origin*. The name of the country of origin is usually required, in English, on all imported products. How the product is labeled, though, can vary. If you're importing stuffed animals, for example, you may be required to have each marked with a label that identifies the country. If your import is a box of pencils, however, you may be required to mark the package, not the individual items. Even the method of labeling can be different. Some products may require a sewn-in label; others, a label glued to the bottom. Proper marking is crucial—a product can be ineligible for sale in the United States if it does not meet the stated requirements.

Tariffs, Duties, and Customs Procedures

For a product to be imported legally, several steps have to occur:

- It must have the proper documentation filled out at entry.
- It must be examined by a customs officer who determines value and suitability for entry.
- The appropriate tariffs or duties must be assigned and paid.
- The process must be reviewed and your goods are given permission to enter. This final step is called "*liquidation.*"

The customs office will provide you with the classification assigned to your product. Information you need, based on your product's classification, includes the rate of duty and marking requirements.

While this is, at best, a rough outline of the procedures, you will need to investigate the specifics of the procedure for your particular situation. Again, the customs office and publications (see chapter 10) are available to help you.

Brokers and Domestic Forwarders

And, for a fee, customhouse brokers are available to help you, too! In the United States, licensed *customhouse brokers* can act as your agent for clearing goods through customs. These brokers deal with the legal requirements and regulations pertaining to importing merchandise. They are a private service, and a customs broker requires a license to assist you in moving your goods. Usually, the broker locates your goods, fills out the necessary entry forms, pays the customs duty (and bills you for it) and then makes arrangements for you to obtain your product. The broker also can make arrangements for any other agencies that need to clear your product. A good broker can advise you on technical requirements for importing, filing entry documents, paying duties, and arranging delivery to your home, office, or warehouse. If the broker delivers the product to you, he or she is also your *domestic freight forwarder*, or the agent who assists you in moving cargo to your domestic destination. There is help for the novice importer, so don't be discouraged if the regulations, restrictions, labeling requirements, and government documentation seem excessive. The reasons for all these regulations are for the safety of our country and our individual consumers. The fact that businesses, large and small, are succeeding at importing is proof that the paperwork does not need to be prohibitive.

Exporting

Let's say those beloved wool-lined slippers are made domestically and you plan to export them. How do you know if Pakistan, or Holland, for that matter, has something similar to our Wool Products Labeling Act, or if they can import wool slippers at all? With exporting, your main concerns are the rules and licensing regulations required abroad. If the foreign importer needs a license to bring your goods into his or her country, or if the product needs to meet certain safety or other requirements, you need to know what the requirements are. You then must make sure the proper paperwork is in place before making any arrangements to ship your item. You need to know the import rules and regulations of foreign countries and those of the U.S. government for export.

Licenses

Most items can be exported from the United States with a general license, which doesn't require an application or preapproval. All you need is to have the license symbol for an Open General License placed in the required spot on the documentation. If your item has military applications or includes new technological innovations, however, the U.S. government will want to control what is sent to other countries, and you will need a *validated export license*. This is applied for through the Department of Commerce. Check there or with the Office of Export Administration to find out whether you need a validated license and, if so, how you should apply for it. The other licensing with which to be concerned when exporting is the foreign country's import license. Find out if they need one, and, if so, how to obtain it. You can call the consulate of that country to find out what they require from you, as exporter, and from your customer, the importer.

Labeling

Just as the United States needs imported items to be labeled with the country of origin, most countries you will export to similarly will require labeling. Often a certificate of origin is required from an exporter, stating "Made in the U.S.A." Your local chamber of commerce will usually certify that your goods are. Contact them to find out what is required.

Freight Forwarders

When exporting, you may want to use the services of a *foreign freight forwarder*. This is a person licensed to help you with the shipping elements of your transaction. He or she can help you book space on ships or aircrafts, arrange for packing, prepare and assemble export documents, and make sure your shipment is put aboard the ship or plane. A good freight forwarder will know the import rules and regulations of foreign countries, and can also tell you what methods of shipping are available to you, what export regulations you need to follow, and what documents are necessary.

Documents

Government agencies, shipping firms, banks, and importing companies have several different documents that are required for each step along the importing and exporting process. Yours may begin with quote requests and contracts, followed by bank drafts and letter of credit forms. The next step may include packing lists, dock receipts, freight bills, and delivery orders. And somewhere along the way you may need import or export licenses, customs entry forms, certificate of origin documents, and inspection reports. Many of these forms are often handled by service firms—brokers, shippers, and freight forwarders—and by government agencies. While the purpose of all these form is to *aid* control, for the beginning importer or exporter the numbers and types of forms may seem overwhelming. As you begin your business, be sure to ask, at each step along the way, what you are required to fill out. Ask when you call customs for product information. Ask again when you speak to your foreign and domestic contacts. Ask your bank, customs broker, freight forwarder, shipper, and anyone else you work with in your transaction. For some transactions the forms will be simple and few; in all cases, the more you put in writing, the safer the transaction will be in terms of preventing misunderstandings and unforeseen circumstances.

Transportation

Shipping and packing are major concerns to importers and exporters. Even if your product is well chosen and well marketed, if it arrives in broken pieces, or is not allowed to enter the country of destination, the success of your business can be at stake. Your responsibilities regarding transporting goods will differ if you are importing or exporting. In both cases, building a successful import/export venture will include:

- becoming familiar with the different types of transportation available to you
- understanding common shipping terms
- realizing the importance of proper packing

Sea, Land or Air?

Choosing the best method for shipping your items, whether bringing them into the country or sending them out, will depend on several factors. Is the shipment large or small? How quickly does it need to arrive? Land transportation is available if you're dealing with customers in Mexico or Canada, but for other countries your choices will be sea or air. For most cases the land transportation aspect, getting your item from or to the border, will be a minor part of the larger importing/exporting picture.

Sea Freight or Air Freight?

For large shipments to most countries, you will need to decide between sea freight or air freight. Sea freight is, of course, slower than air freight, and thus cheaper. The proper analysis will take these factors into account when choosing the best means for your product. Less expensive is not always better. Once you decide on sea or air travel, you have several other choices to make. In sea travel you can choose between scheduled, non-scheduled, or charter services. For air travel you can choose between passenger flights, all-cargo flights, or charter flights. Researching the costs and time differentials among the different options should help you choose the best method for your particular business transaction.

Air Mail or Sea Mail?

Small quantities can be sent through air or sea mail. For shipments that do not exceed certain dollar amounts (currently shipments which do not go over $1000 in value, but check with the post office for specifics), items received by mail will be moved through customs by the postal department, which submits the package for customs examination. A customs officer fills out a mail entry form. The package is delivered and, if any duty is shown due on the mail entry, the addressee must pay it to retain the package. This can save you from having to hire a customs broker or freight forwarder, and can save you time in filling out documents. A mail shipment which exceeds the specified limit will be forwarded to the customs office nearest the destination of the address on the package. You then would have to go to that office and fill out an entry form in order to receive the package. The major disadvantages to air or sea mail are that restrictions on size and weight are limited. Also, the maximum amount of money for which you can insure your shipment is relatively small. Again, figuring out the total cost will be your best approach to choosing the right transportation service for your business.

⎧ Shipping Terms

Many of the more common terms you will hear when people discuss international trade are those that refer to shipping. Even if you use freight forwarders and custom brokers to do much of the paperwork, you need to understand the terms applied to international trade to build a thriving business.

Multimodel transportation refers to goods that use more than one method of transportation in getting from one destination to another. If your plexiglass picture frames are being exported from a manufacturer in Denver to an importer in Paris, the shipment may include rail travel to New York, sea travel to LeHavre or Marseilles, and air travel to Paris. Other terms you will hear are *FOB*, *FAS*, *C&F* and *CIF*. These terms describe the way the product will be handled through shipment, who (the importer or the exporter) will be responsible for different aspects of the transaction, and who will be responsible for insurance, cost, and freight.

FOB   FOB means "Free On Board." This indicates that the risk of loss or damage to the goods is transferred from the seller to the buyer when the goods are placed "on board" the ship.

FOB airport   This is similar to the FOB term, indicating that risk of loss or damage to the goods is transferred from the seller to the buyer when the goods have been delivered to the air carrier at the airport of departure. Once the goods are considered to be "on board" a plane, the title passes to the importer.

FAS   FAS indicates "Free Alongside Ship." This means the seller's obligations are fulfilled when the goods have been placed alongside the ship. The difference from FOB is that the exporter is responsible for goods up until the point at which it is ready to be loaded on the ship. The title changes hands when the shipment is "alongside the ship," not necessarily "on board." Although this distinction seems almost incidental, the freight forwarding charges, export taxes, loading charges, and other costs occur *after* "alongside ship" and *before* "on board."

C&F C&F stands for "Cost and Freight." When this term is used, the exporter, or seller, pays the cost and freight necessary to bring the goods to the destination. Insurance, however, is in the hands of the importer, or buyer, and the risk of loss or damage to the goods is transferred to the importer from the time the goods are on board the ship.

CIF CIF means "Cost, Insurance and Freight." This term means that the exporter not only pays the cost and freight but includes insurance costs as well. Therefore the risk of loss or damage to the goods in transit is the responsibility of the seller.

Packing

How important is the packing procedure you choose? Think about your shipment of feather dusters being imported from Norway. If not packed properly, how will they travel across the sea with a heavy shipment of five-pound barbells resting on top of them? If you are importing, determine how your products arrive and make sure the packing done by your overseas distributor is adequate. You don't want it to be either too weak, and therefore susceptible to damage when jostled around in transport, or too heavy, making it more expensive then necessary to ship. If you are an exporter, be sure your domestic manufacturer of the products you are sending knows how to pack and mark the boxes for overseas travel. You can also pay specialized export packing companies to prepare your shipment for safe travel. What are you are hoping to prevent through proper packing and marking of the package?

- breakage
- moisture or temperature damage
- improper handling
- pilferage

Find the best packing and sealing materials for your particular shipment to protect against damage. Choose a waterproof container that will prevent water or moisture damage. And remember to mark your box with the appropriate warnings in appropriate languages (OPEN THIS END, for example, or FRAGILE–GLASS). These important steps can help save you time and money.

International Payment

Like shipping terms, familiarity with international payment terms allows you to begin importing and exporting from a solid base of information. Understanding the costs, advantages, and risks of each method will help you decide which will work for your transaction. You also need information on finding a bank that can handle import or export transactions. Even a small import or export business will use specialized international payment processes. Your bankers should have the department and staff to handle the documentation properly and efficiently.

Banks

Look for a bank with a strong international department that can easily handle transactions. Some banks have corresponding relationships with those in other countries. Find out what banks, if any, have this kind of reciprocal arrangement in the country with which you are planning to do your importing or exporting. Your bank should also be able to check your supplier's or customer's bank references.

Methods of Payment

Different methods of payment exist which vary in terms of risk to the importer or exporter. It would be wonderful if you could arrange with your distributor in Taiwan, for instance, to send you a shipment of goods with the agreement that you would pay for it when you have received money from your customer, if you are an import agent, or when you have sold the items directly, if you are an import merchant. For a small, first-time import or export transaction, however, it is unlikely that you will be "trusted" to make good on your end of the deal. Would you, as an exporter, send a shipment of bicycles to a foreign country and agree to wait until the person at the other end has sold the bicycles and received payment before you would get any money? It's not the safest way to do business. Different methods of payment, to facilitate the process of getting paid for goods and services in international transactions, were designed to protect domestic and foreign importers and exporters. The most common method used in international trade are:

- open account
- bill of exchange
- letter of credit
- payment in advance
- consignment

Open Account

You may be familiar with open accounts through the domestic transactions in many companies. The person sending the goods, the exporter, ships them and sends an invoice after the shipment. The importer, the person receiving the goods, has thirty days or so to pay. The main difference from domestic transactions is that you would send (or receive) an international money order or bank check to pay the bill. The risk to the importer is low, but the risk to the exporter is high. Depending on which side of the deal you are on, you must decide if this method is acceptable. If you are just beginning to import, it may be difficult to find foreign distributors willing to send you goods in this manner. As a new exporter, however, you may be asked to send goods on an open account, and you'll need to carefully weigh the risks involved.

Bill of Exchange

A bill of exchange is a document that is signed by the seller and addressed to the importer, ordering him or her to pay the amount indicated on the document. The person exporting, or selling the merchandise, initiates the payment process. The bill of exchange, sometimes referred to as a draft, is prepared and presented to the buyer from the domestic bank to the foreign one. Once the buyer at the other end signs the draft, the bank takes money from the buyer's account and transfers it to the seller's account. In some instances, the importer can pick up the merchandise without having to pay for it until a later date. If a *bill of lading* is issued, this document serves as title to the merchandise, making it necessary for the importer to agree to the bill of exchange once the merchandise is accepted. This means once the importer signs to accept the merchandise, he or she is also agreeing to the bill of exchange, and the bank is permitted to transfer money from your account to the exporter's. Drafts can be issued with specific requirements, and you should agree on the exact terms with your supplier or buyer.

Letter of Credit

With a letter of credit, or LC, the buyer, or importer, is responsible for the payment process. The seller requests that the buyer furnishes a letter of credit—a letter from the importer's bank, stating that payment is guaranteed upon presentation of certain documents. Why would the bank agree to guarantee your payment? Usually because it has ensured that you can pay it, either by an account you have at that bank that covers the amount of the payment, or some other method that it used to confidently offer you this credit line. It's much like other forms of credit you may have. As with revolving credit or credit cards, you need to find out what your bank offers and what its additional charges will be, over and above the actual payment to the supplier of the merchandise.

Consignment

Consignment offers a different sort of payment arrangement. The importer takes possession of the product, but does not take title. A percentage of the actual sale is then paid to the exporter. Suppose you owned a bridal gown shop and wanted to put on display in your shop some original but very expensive bridal gowns that you saw in Sweden. You couldn't afford to buy them outright, but you asked to import them on consignment, and agreed to pay the exporter a percentage of any sales you made. The exporter may agree to this deal if he or she feels that exposure of the gowns in the United States might be worthwhile, or if the gowns are not selling at all in his or her own ship. You may export on consignment if the reverse is true—your product is simply not selling domestically and you want to try it in a foreign market. If you use this method, be sure to follow through with possible outcomes. What will you do if the product never sells? What happens if it's lost or damaged? How will you make sure you are getting the agreed upon percentage of sales? At what point will you have the items returned to their owner?

Paying in Advance

If you are importing chocolate bars from Sweden and you prepay the entire shipment, you are using a *payment in advance*. As long as you trust your supplier in Sweden, you could send an international money order and simply buy the chocolate bars outright. Sometimes you can agree to pay half, similar to a deposit, and then send that amount in an international money order. This saves time and sometimes money, provided the merchandise arrives on time and in the agreed upon condition. You avoid applying for letters of credit or establishing an arrangement with an international bank. Any international bank can issue you a money order if you give it, in cash, the amount required plus a service fee. As an exporter, you may ask the buyer to send you all or part of the money in advance through this method. Once you receive the check or money order and have verified it with your bank, you ship the goods. This is probably the simplest, most straightforward method of payment. If you are distrustful of the shipper, however, or if the shipper is distrustful of you, this method may be difficult to arrange.

Foreign Currency

Will you always be paying or receiving payment in U.S. dollars? The answer to this question depends in part on the value of the dollar—when it is good, everyone wants it, when it is low, other currencies are more valued. As an importer, you most likely will not be asked to pay in currency other than your own. If you are exporting, however, you may be asked to take payment in foreign currency.

What should you do? Your first step would be to check with your bank to determine the value of that country's currency, and figure out how much, by the exchange rate standards, you will make on the deal. You might then agree to accept foreign currency at a higher rate so that you will still make the amount, in U.S. dollars, for which you negotiated in the first place. Exchange rates fluctuate rapidly, though, and you may not be able to determine what the value of the foreign currency will be when the payment is made. Some arrangements will be far more risky than others. If you know the country to be economically stable and you know you are able to exchange the money easily, accepting foreign currency may actually be in your favor.

Summary

Buying and selling in the international market is not that different from buying and selling domestically. You just need to know a few more rules, a few more terms, a few more facts about international currency, and a few more regulatory agencies and requirements. There is plenty of help from private services which, for a fee, will handle most, if not all, of the international documentation, shipping arrangements, and financial details. Once you realize *what* you need to know and *where* you can get the necessary information, the specifics of international trade are simply another step in building your successful business.

C&V officers   Classification and Value officers; the people at customs who are responsible for the legal determination of your product and how much duty should get charged.

Liquidation   The final step in the importing process where required import information is reviewed. If the information and documents are accepted, the merchandise is considered liquidated.

Validated export license A government permit required to export specific items to specific countries.

Foreign freight forwarder The agent who assists the exporter in moving shipments to a foreign destination.

Multimodel transportation Goods that use more than one method of transportation in movement between countries (i.e., rail, air, sea).

TSUS Tariff Schedule of the United States.

FOB Free on Board (a shipping term).

FAS Free Alongside Ship (a shipping term).

C&F Cost and Freight (a shipping term).

CIF Cost, Insurance and Freight (a shipping term).

LC Letter of Credit (a payment term).

8 | *International Travel*

If you are entering the import/export business because you love to travel, this chapter may reinforce your reasons for wanting to spend time abroad. For a less-than-enthusiastic traveler, the advantage of transacting business deals in-person is often a good enough incentive to go. Add to this the importance of inspecting manufacturing plants, checking up on the salespeople, and seeing first hand what is happening "on-site" at ports of entry or destination, and you'll have more than enough reason to pack your bags and take off. Flying regularly to Europe, the Middle East, or wherever you choose to do business can and often *should* become a part of your import/export lifestyle. Knowing the basics of the travel field—passports, visa, customs, tax deductions—can help you enjoy the international travel bonuses of the import and export world.

Planning Your Trip

Are you planning to "shop" for items to import on your trip? Will you be meeting with buyers or sellers, hoping to begin the deal-making process? Do you intend to visit several stores to see where your exports could be marketed?

Determining the goals of each trip will help you decide upon several factors in its "before" stages. Planning the details of your trip—how long to stay, where to stay, best times to arrive and depart, what clothes to bring, etc.—will differ depending on your specific goals. If you're planning to meet with potential customers, for example, you need to allow ample time for negotiations. You may also want to bring appropriate business clothing, rather than the more comfortable, casual wear vacationers usually take. If on-site checks of buyers' or sellers' facilities are your aim, it may be important to figure in distance from manufacturers' plants, transportation options, hours of operation, and available personnel to assist you in an on-site visit. Perhaps your plan is to visit artist colonies and open markets. Do you know if the country you intend to visit has specific days of the week when flea markets or craft fairs are in operation? Answering questions like this can help you better choose what countries to visit, when to go, how long to stay, and what clothing you should bring. Major sources for information on travel to and around the country you plan to visit are government tourist offices, travel books, and travel agents.

Passport

You'll need a passport for travel to almost all foreign countries. It identifies you as a citizen of the country in which it is issued. The typical U.S. passport issued to adults is valid for ten years and has twenty-four pages. If you plan on traveling extensively, you can request a forty-eight- or ninety-six-page passport. You can apply for one in person at U.S. Passport Agency offices, local county courthouses, and some selected post offices. Although there are ways to rush the procedure, you should allow about four to six weeks for processing your application. Remember that you'll need to show your passport when you enter or leave most countries. If your passport is lost or stolen while abroad, report this immediately to local authorities and apply for a replacement at the nearest United States Embassy or consular office.

Visa

Some countries require a *visa*, an official endorsement made on your passport, noting that you are given official permission to enter that country. Your travel agent or local consulate office can let you know if you need one.

Currency

In addition to the usual decisions regarding cash, credit cards, travelers checks, and currency exchange information, you may want to find out how to do cash transfers from overseas. If you're looking for imports and find items you don't want to leave behind, the only way to secure the purchase may be to provide cash on the spot. Depending on where you are and who you are buying from, credit cards may not be an option.

Tax-Deductible Status

Your trip to Hong Kong or Afghanistan can be a tax-deductible expense if it involves activities related to your import/export business. Did your trip involve:

- meeting with business contacts?
- attending work-related meetings?
- negotiating a contract?
- doing work-related research?

The expenses incurred for these activities may be deducted as travel expenses. Keep good records during your travels. Make sure your receipts show that you are actually doing business. The Internal Revenue Service may look very closely at travel expenses, and you need to be able to substantiate any claim you make. Talk to a good accountant, tax attorney, or tax consultant to get the help you need.

Customs Officials

When you return from your trip, be aware that the U.S. Customs personnel have the legal right to examine every piece of luggage you carry in. Under the spot-check system you may get by without any more than a glance, but you should be prepared if you do get inspected. In most instances, up to $400 worth of foreign merchandise as gifts or for personal use—not for resale—may be brought in duty-free by U.S. residents provided they have been out of the country more than forty-eight hours, and provided they have not claimed a similar exemption within the previous thirty days. For the next $1,000 worth of merchandise, a flat 10 percent is assessed. A gift costing less than $40 may be mailed from abroad on a duty-free basis, as long as it is marked "unsolicited gift—value under $50," and no one person receives more than one such gift in one day. For items over these dollar amounts, or products you intend to sell, you will need to pay appropriate duties and make a written declaration. To get business samples and other business equipment through customs, you may want to use a special customs document created to aid professional travelers. Apply to the Council for International Business for more information on the specific requirements and fees associated with these documents.

Summary

Opportunities for travel as a business expense are abundant. Any successful import/export operation will require substantial communication with individuals and companies overseas, and traveling to personally meet the people with whom you are doing business is an excellent way to stay on top of your international transactions. By planning your trip for business, not simply for pleasure where you may or may not find some interesting items to import, you will be better prepared to handle the specific situations which an importer or exporter may encounter. Preparation is the key—knowing what to plan for can turn the often pleasurable act of international travel into an integral part of your import/export business.

Passport A formal document issued by an authorized agency of a country to one of its citizens. Usually necessary for exit from and reentry into the country.

Visa An endorsement made on a passport by the proper authorities noting that it has been examined and that the bearer may proceed.

9 | *Administrative Tasks*

Making your business a reality involves many specific tasks, from registering your company name and printing stationery to discovering your options for international communications. An important function in *any* business is administration and office management, and a business that deals in trade across international borders requires a relatively high amount of attention to details. Knowing what is involved in starting your own business can help you decide how to begin implementing your own import or export ideas.

Starting a Business

What turns my import or export ideas into a "business"?
Do I need to fill out any special paperwork?
Can I start a small business out of my home?
Are there tax implications to my choices?
What kind of equipment do I need to start?

Answers to these questions will vary from person to person, business to business, depending on factors such as the size of your business, number of employees, type of product you will be importing or exporting, and even where you live. Knowing your options, however, will help you make a good "fit" between the business choices available and the particular needs of your import/export operation.

What Turns My Ideas Into a Business?

Deciding how to organize your business is the first step in turning your ideas into reality. The three common forms of business organizations are *sole proprietorship, partnership,* and *corporation.* You should select the right form for your business based on the intent of your enterprise, tax implications, liability requirements, and costs involved. You may want to consult a lawyer to figure out which is the right choice for you.

Sole Proprietorship

This is probably the simplest form, and one of the most popular with beginning importers and exporters. If you will be the sole owner of the company, and see little need for taking on the paperwork and reporting requirements of a corporation, you may want to choose this for your business. At income tax time, you simply show your self-employment income on an IRS Schedule C. You also list your expenses and determine your profit or loss. This amount combines with your employment income for tax declaration. Check with your county and state to see if any type of permit, registration, or license is required.

Partnership

Also popular with start-up import/export businesses is a partnership. This indicates there is more than one owner, and each partner declares his or her expenses, profits or losses on the income tax return. In a limited partnership, the limited partner is usually involved in the financial aspects of the business but not the management. Again, check locally and with your state to see if there is a particular process required for registering your business or filing a statement of partnership.

Corporation

Should you incorporate? You need to weigh the tax advantages and liability protection options against the accounting requirements when deciding whether this is a good choice for your business. As an individual you would share in the liability if any harm is caused in the distribution of your product. As a corporation, your liability is usually limited to its assets. You will need to file papers with the appropriate government offices, so you'll probably want to do a little more research or check with a lawyer to find out your state's requirements and the proper steps to proceed.

Office Space: Working From Home

The import/export business can be ideal for people who want to work from home. Depending on the nature and volume of your transactions, the only "office equipment" you may need are a telephone and a typewriter or a PC. Clear a space on your desk or table, set up a file or two, and you're in business! Especially for those who want to start out on a part-time basis, working from home may be the perfect choice. As your business grows, you may need more employees, a separate phone, and larger space in which to do business. And the specifics of your business—if you're importing life-size wooden giraffes from Africa, for example—will dictate your particular needs. As your business grows in complexity and volume, you may want to rethink your office needs. Be sure to check the laws in your area concerning using one's home for business purposes. There may be restrictions on number of employees, number of business visitors, and the stocking of merchandise. If you are working by yourself, however, and have no reason to expect business visitors, you should have no trouble at all meeting the requirements.

Expenses

A good business plan will include:

- your objectives
- your marketing plan
- an accurate accounting of your resources
- your implementation strategies

Exploring these areas will help you figure out your expenses. Even a small business has substantial start-up costs—telephone, answering machine, stationery—and dealing with international phone calls and telexes can be costly. How many of the following items will your business need?

Office space	Telex
Rent	Postage meter
Copier	Typewriter
Telephone	P.O. box
Answering machine	Filing cabinets
An 800 number	Envelopes
Stationery	Shipping boxes
Computer	Postage scale
Checking account	Office furniture
Business cards	Long distance phone
Fax machine	service
Inventory	Accordion files
Calculator	Computer Printer

Communications

Since you won't always be able to travel to Australia to check up on your lollipop exporting business, you'll probably want to find a fast, inexpensive, and easily accessible way to communicate with your buyers and sellers. The proliferation of facsimile (fax) machines, competitive long-distance phone services, and advanced computer technology have made communicating internationally easier and more efficient then ever before. Today you can pick up the phone and dial most countries direct. You can fax a drawing or illustration of a product's specifications and have a copy show up within minutes at your overseas destination. From your personal computer in the basement of your Los Angeles home, you can send an electronic message to your exporter's office in London. Personal computers and fax machines are not only becoming more affordable but increasing their capacity to do the kind of communicating importers and exporters need. As faxes and computers continue to grow in popularity, your choices for international communications may become easier. Currently, however, you still need to accept the fact that there are places around the world where a fax or electronic mail message may have trouble finding its intended destination.

Telephone

While computer enthusiasts may argue that electronic mail, bulletin boards, and on-line computer services are making human contact unnecessary, the power of speaking directly to a human being—and getting a live voice in response—is hardly relinquishing its role as the preferred means of immediate, direct communication. It's often the fastest way to convey ideas and solve last-minute problems. You'll probably want to investigate the different long-distance carriers to determine which have the best service to the foreign countries you'll want to contact.

Mailing Address

If you're working out of your home and don't want to give away your personal address, you may want to consider post office boxes. Many larger cities also have mail box services which generally have prestigious addresses and will receive your mail for you. If you're dealing with a country that interprets a post office address as a sign of instability, these mail box services may be a better alternative.

Telex or Fax?

Fax machines transmit images, often in a matter of seconds. They are the fastest growing method of communications. There also are a growing number of communication services which offer fax services. As the cost of fax machines, both for business and personal use, continues to drop, you'll hear an ever larger number of people telling you to "Just fax it to me."

Telex

Telex is a system of electronic communication, and has been the most popular method of international communications. It has virtually replaced the cable, or international telegram, for most overseas contact. You can send and receive telexes by using a telex service or buying telecommunications software for your computer. You could also buy or rent a telex machine, which, like a computer, connects through a telephone line to send and receive your messages. The choice between telex or fax is generally a question of accessibility to the person with whom you're communicating. Depending on the country, you may rely more heavily on one or the other for fast communication. Often the decision is easy—many foreign countries, especially Third World countries, still rely heavily on telex.

Summary

Choosing the right office, equipment, and communications system will depend a lot on what you're looking for. Is your goal to spend as little time and money as possible? Will you "make do" with what you already have? Is it important for you to have top-of-the-line, up-to-date equipment? Starting a business is simply that—*starting*—and your choices and decision will change as your business needs grow and change. While it's important, and often fun, to spend time designing business cards and buying a computer, keep in mind that the administrative end of your business is only one aspect of it. All areas of importing and exporting—purchasing, marketing, international trade and travel—need to come together to help make your business a successful one.

TELEX   An electronic communications service.

FAX   A facsimile; the electronic transmission of the facsimile.

10 | *Where Can I Get More Information?*

Now that you know *what* kind of information you need to start your own import/export business, the next important step is finding out *where* you can get this information. Many references have been made to government sources such as the Department of Commerce and the International Trade Administration. This chapter will tell you how to find the offices nearest you. For specific information about regulations, business transactions, travel documents, marketing plans, and more, you'll find names and publishers of books, pamphlets, and other valuable sources of information included here as well. You probably will want to start at your local library—most of the publications mentioned here will be found at a good one.

Chapter 1: Starting an Import/Export Business

Two of the most valuable sources for finding out more about the import/export business are published by the government. *Importing Into the United States* (approx. $4.50) and *A Basic Guide to Exporting* (approx. $8.50) are both available by mail from the Government Printing Office, Washington, D.C. 20229. (202) 783-3238. Ask for their catalog of publications. You could also visit one of the twenty-four government bookstores (most are open Monday through Friday) and browse through the publications available to help you import or export. The New York bookstore is at 26 Federal Plaza; the phone number is (212) 264-3825. For the store closest to you call information, the New York number, or the Washington, D.C., bookstore, (202) 275-2091.

Chapter 2: Are You Right for This Business?

To determine if you'd be happy in the import/export business, you may want to start getting some publications that deal with international issues. A good choice is *Global Trade Executive*, published by North American Publishing Co. in Philadelphia. You'll also find specific import and export opportunities listed here. Joining an association, such as the American Association of Importers and Exporters, (212) 944-2230, is another way to find out what kind of people and organizations are doing business in international trade.

Chapter 3: Purchasing: What Will I Import?

To find out where trade shows are being held, you may want to order the *Trade Shows and Professional Exhibits Directory* from Gale Research Company in Detroit. Another source is the *Trade Show and Convention Guide*, published by Amusement Business in Nashville. For a list of United States manufacturers, check the *Thomas Register of American Manufacturers* available from the Thomas Publishing Company, New York. Another good source is *Major Mass-Market Merchandisers*, published by the Salesman's Guide, New York. If you are looking for products to import, try subscribing to trade publications. *Trade Channel*, available from American Business Communications, (914) 631–1802; *Asian Sources*, from Wordwright Enterprises, (312) 475-1900; and *Made in Europe*, (212) 243-3130, are three popular sources. Another magazine that deals with low-priced and novelty items to import is the *International Intertrade Index*, (201) 682-2382. You'll probably also want to contact the *U.S. Customs Office*, once you've chosen your product, to find out the duty on it, how it has to be labeled, and what restrictions might pertain, (202) 566-8511, for the office nearest you.

Chapter 4: Purchasing: What Will I Export?

Dun and Bradstreet's *Exporters Encyclopedia* is a good source for information about technical specifications, such as electrical characteristics, for each country. *Thomas Register of American Manufacturers* is a good resource of manufacturers and so is the *Directory of Manufacturers Representatives*, published by McGraw-Hill, New York. Also try the *Encyclopedia of Associations* by Gale Research Company, (1-800) 223-GALE, which provides a list of American and international manufacturer's associations. The *International Trade Administration (ITA)* is part of the Department of Commerce and supports exporting. There is an office in almost every state. For information about U.S. and foreign commercial service posts, call (202) 377-1599.

Chapter 5: Marketing: Where Do I Sell My Imports?

The *Journal of Commerce* puts out a *Directory of U.S. Importers* which can help you find companies that import. Some sources for mail order and flea market information are *Facts on File Directory of Mail Order Catalogs* (New York), *Marketers Forum*, and *National Flea Market Dealer* (Florida).

Chapter 6: Marketing: Where Do I Sell My Exports?

The *Philadelphia Export Directory*, published by Philadelphia Export Network, is one helpful source for export information. Also try the magazine *Global Trade Executive*. The U.S. Department of Commerce publishes a monthly magazine called *Business America* which also may be helpful.

Chapter 7: International Trade

The Customs Office will be your first source of information for finding out specific regulations concerning your importing/exporting business. To find out about export licenses, contact the *Office of Export Administration* at Box 273, Washington, D.C. 20044. For information about shipping terms, try *Guide to INCOTERMS*, published by ICC Publishing Corporation, New York, which will help you understand the responsibilities of the importer and exporter under each term. To find out more about documents used in international trade, look at *Sourcebook*, from Unz & Co., (1-800) 631-3098. Another source for information may be your international bank. Marine Midland Bank publishes *Introduction to International Banking Services*, and many international banks offer free books on trade finance.

Chapter 8: International Travel

To get a passport you can make application to a passport agency (located in Boston, Chicago, Honolulu, Houston, Los Angeles, Miami, New Orleans, New York, Philadelphia, San Francisco, Seattle, Stamford, Conn., and Washington, D.C.) as well as some post offices and some federal and state courts. If you lose your passport in the United States, contact Passport Services, 1425 K Street, N.W., Washington, D.C., or the nearest passport agency. Overseas, report loss or theft to the nearest U.S. Embassy or consulate. You may want to check with the Citizens Emergency Center, Washington, D.C., at (202) 647-5225 to find out possible danger areas around the world. A government publication, *Your Trip Abroad*, available from the Government Printing Office in Washington, D.C., gives additional information on loss and theft of a passport as well as other travel tips.

Chapter 9: Administrative Tasks

Check out the magazine *Global Trade Executive* for information on trade procedures. Contact the Internal Revenue Service, a bureau of the U.S. Treasury Department, for up-to-date information on tax exemptions and deductions that apply to your particular business situation. *A Guide to Export Documentation* from Educational Development for International Trade, Dayton, Ohio, can help you learn more about the paperwork involved in exporting and importing.

Summary

Baskets from Brazil, flowers from France, hats to Haiti—the possibilities are endless. You now know what to look for in a product, a market, and a bank. You know how to determine what kind of business is for you. With the questions raised in the first nine chapters, and the sources for answers listed in this one, you are ready to begin your career in international trade. There's never been a better time to combine your love of travel, your business sense, your shopping expertise, and your management capabilities into a profitable import/export business. Good luck!

Glossary

Agent One who acts for, or in the place of another as, a representative.

C&F C&F stands for "Cost and Freight." When this term is used, the exporter, or seller, pays the cost and freight necessary to bring the goods to the destination. Insurance, however, is in the hands of the importer, or buyer, and the risk of loss or damage to the goods is transferred to the importer from the time the goods are on board the ship.

C&V officers Classification and Value officers, who are the people at customs who are responsible for determining the legal determination of your product and how much duty should get charged.

CIF CIF means "Cost, Insurance and Freight." This term means that the exporter not only pays the cost and freight but includes insurance costs as well. Therefore the risk of loss or damage to the goods in transit is the responsibility of the seller.

Commission A fee paid to an agent for transacting a piece of business or performing a service (usually a percentage of the money received from a total paid to the agent responsible for the business).

Consumer products Goods that directly satisfy human wants.

Currency The medium of exchange or barter.

Customs The procedures and organization involved in the collection of duties levied by a country on imports and exports.

Demographics The statistical characteristics of populations (such as age and income) used to identify markets.

Department of Commerce The agency of government whose purpose it is to promote commercial industrial interests in the country.

Export merchant A merchant who sells directly to a foreign purchaser (not using a middleperson).

Exporting The sending of goods to another country or overseas territory.

FAS FAS means "Free Alongside Ship." This means the seller's obligations are fulfilled when the goods have been placed alongside the ship. The difference from FOB is that the exporter is responsible for goods up until the point at which it is ready to be loaded on the ship. The title changes hands when the shipment is "alongside the ship," not necessarily "on board." Although this distinction seems almost incidental, the freight forwarding charges, export taxed, loading charges and other costs occur *after* "alongside ship" and *before* "on board".

Fax A facsimile; the electronic transmission of the facsimile.

FOB FOB means "Free on Board." This indicates that the risk of loss or damage to the goods is transferred from the seller to the buyer when the goods are placed "on board" the ship.

FOB airport This is similar to the FOB term, indicating that risk of loss or damage to the goods is transferred from the seller to the buyer when the goods have been delivered to the air carrier at the airport of departure. Once the goods are considered to be "on board" a plane, the title passes to the importer.

Foreign freight forwarder The agent who assists the exporter in moving shipments to a foreign destination.

Foreign sales agent/representative One who serves as the foreign representative of a domestic supplier and tries to obtain sales abroad for that supplier.

Importing When goods are brought into a country from another country or overseas territory.

Industrial products Goods that are used in industry.

International trade When the goods or services offered by someone are exchanged for currency or the goods and services offered by someone else, and this exchange takes place across international boundaries.

LC Letter of Credit (a payment term).

License or permit A permission granted by government authority to engage in an import or export business.

Liquidation The final step in the importing process where required import information is reviewed. If the information and documents are accepted, the merchandise is considered liquidated.

Market indicators Any of a group of statistical values that taken together give an indication of the market.

Merchant A buyer and seller of commodities for profit.

Multimodel transportation Goods that use more than one method of transportation in movement between countries (i.e., rail, air, sea).

Passport A formal document issued by an authorized official of a country to one of its citizens. Usually necessary for exit from and reentry into the country.

Quota The total quantity of a product which may be imported into a country without restriction or additional duties or taxes.

Sales representative A representative who acts as a salesman, usually for a commission.

Tariffs Duties imposed by a government on goods imported or exported.

Telex An electronic communications service.

TSUS Tariff Schedule of the United States.

Validated export license A permit, from the government, required to export specific items to specific countries.

Visa An endorsement made on a passport by the proper authorities denoting that it has been examined and that the bearer may proceed.

Index